WITHDRAWN

ROUTE 6

Paul Blum

RISING ★ STARS

Rising Stars UK Ltd.
22 Grafton Street, London W1S 4EX
www.risingstars-uk.com

nasen

NASEN House, 4/5 Amber Business Village, Amber Close,
Amington, Tamworth, Staffordshire B77 4RP

Published 2008

Cover design: pentacorbig
Illustrator: Chris King, Illustration Ltd.
Text design and typesetting: pentacorbig
Publisher: Gill Budgell
Editor: Catherine Baker
Editorial project management: Margot O'Keeffe
Editorial consultant: Lorraine Petersen
Photos: Alamy, p35 Samuel Ralli

British Library Cataloguing in Publication Data.
A CIP record for this book is available from the British Library.

ISBN: 978-1-84680-454-0

Printed by Craft Print International Limited, Singapore

shadows

Contents

The Crash

- The Crash happened in 2021. Alien space ships crash landed on Earth.

- After The Crash, the Earth became very cold and dark.

- Now the aliens rule the world.

- The aliens have changed shape so they look like people.

- People call the aliens The Enemy.

Life after the Crash

- People are afraid.

- They do not know who is an Enemy and who is a friend.

The Firm

- The Firm keeps order on the streets.

- The Firm keeps people safe from Enemy attacks.

About Matt Merton

Matt Merton works for The Firm. He often works with Dexter. Their job is to find and kill The Enemy. They use Truth Sticks to do this.

But Matt has problems.

Matt has lost his memory. He cannot answer some big questions.

- Where has Jane, his girlfriend, gone?

- How did he get his job with The Firm?

Matt thinks The Firm is on the side of good. But is it?

chapter 1

It was a cold night. The snow was falling.
Matt Merton went into the bar.

'I need a coffee, Sam,' he said. 'With an extra shot, and extra hot.'

'An extra shot, and extra hot. Coming right up,' said Sam.

'Hey — a woman left this for you.' Sam gave Matt
a letter.

'The woman said her name was Jane,' said Sam.
'She said you know who she is.'

'Jane!' said Matt. 'She was here? In the bar?'

'Yes,' said Sam. 'About an hour ago.'

Matt opened the letter.

'Route Six?' said Matt. 'See you, Sam. I've got to go.'

Matt,

Find Route Six.
You need to remember
everything. Then maybe
you can see me again.

Jane

'Hey,' said Sam. 'What about your coffee?'

'No time for coffee,' said Matt. 'I've got work to do.'

chapter 2

Matt got on the sky tram.

He went to The Firm.

It was very late. There was nobody about.

Matt did not go to his office. He went to the Head of The Firm's office.

He broke the lock on the door.

Matt typed the words 'Route Six' on the computer.

But the computer crashed.

'No good!' said Matt. 'It's a dead end!'

Then Matt had an idea. He broke the lock on the desk.

There were paper files.

In the paper files, Matt found a file about Jane.

It was very thick. The Firm knew a lot about her.

But the Firm did not know where Jane was. She was still missing.

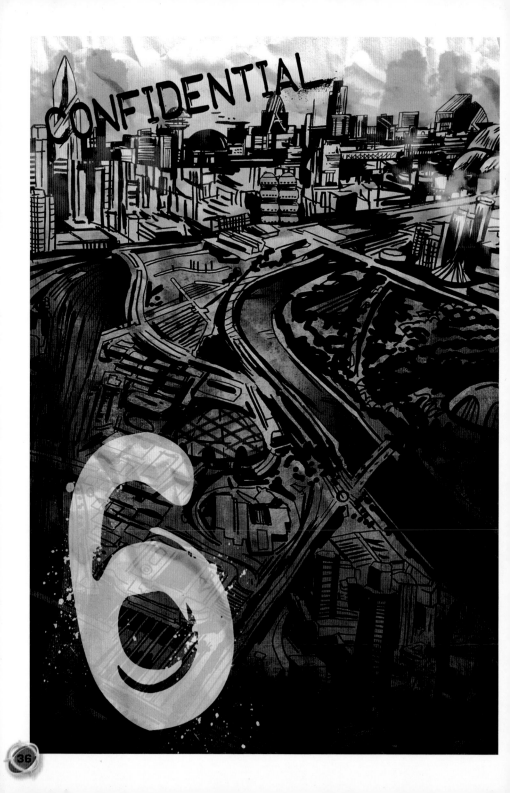

Matt found a map in Jane's file.

Was this a map of Route Six? Matt had to find out.

chapter 3

Matt went to the north of the city. He went to the area shown on the map.

He watched and waited.

Many trucks came past.

They held hundreds of people. The people looked
very sad.

The people could not get off the trucks. There were bars on all the windows.

'Where are you going?' Matt shouted.

But they could not hear him.

Matt watched the trucks leave. He did not know what was happening.

Matt walked back across the city.

It was a long way.

Matt just walked with his head down.

His mind was racing.

There were so many questions.

Where was Jane?

Why was The Firm so interested in her?

What did Matt's boss know about the people on the trucks?

Matt had to find out.

about the author

AUTHOR NAME
Paul Blum

JOB
Teacher

LAST KNOWN LOCATION
North London, England

NOTES
Before The Crash taught in Inner-city London
schools. Writer of series of books called
The Extraordinary Files. Believed to be in
hiding from The Firm. Wanted for questioning.
Seems to know more about The Enemy than
he should ...